Marion (Kalinowski) Sadler

Poems?

Poems ?
Poems ?
Poems ?
Poems ?
Poems ?
?

Poems? Poems? Poem? Poems?

PUBLISHING HISTORY

First Printing Trade Paperback Edition Published 2015

All Rights Reserved
Copyright © 2015 by Mary Ann Kalin

No part of this publication may be reproduced, stored in a retrieval system or transmitted in any form or by any means, electronic, mechanical, photocopying, recording, scanning, printing, or otherwise, except as permitted under Sections 107 or 108 of the 1976 United States Copyright Act, without either the prior written permission of the Publisher or Author. Requests to the Publisher or Author for permission should be addressed to: Twilight Art and Book Publishers, Addison, IL. 60101, e-mail: tweditorsrm@gmail.com, phone: (630) 780-2454.

ISBN-13: 978-1530611751
ISBN-10: 153061175X

Printed in The United States of America

I dedicate this book to my children, and my long time friends; Barbara Peterson, Delores Standaret, Alberta Tague, Doris Bonnewell, Linda Willard

Preface

I have written about the State of Tennessee and how it has inspired me in both poem and prose, and perhaps some in between.

Everyone has a favorite place they like to get to, go to, at home, a comfortable piece of furniture, a favorite dish, desert or a particular outfit to wear. I could go on.

Places that we are born in or those we move to; we need to appreciate the people and the state. We must be pleasant and kind to those that live there and respectful of the state, traditions, and customs - their culture.

The culture might be different from state to state, but people are the same in many ways. The love and enjoyment they have of family and friends.

We love laugh and can enjoy ourselves to the very end of our time here on earth. What a good life we have.

Acknowledgements

  I consulted with my oldest son for all his help in getting together this book of poems. He has the knowledge and understanding of the writ-ten word. I thank him for all his help in putting these poems into book form.

  I want to thank my husband for his patience and understanding for the time I spent at the computer and on phone consulting with my son and reading my written words to see if they made sense.

Thanks to "Art Finishing" for the use of their vector graphics of fireworks on the front cover. www.artvectors.com.

x

Introduction

My home state was Wisconsin. This is where I met my first husband on a blind date. At the time he was in the Air Force and happened to be stationed at the Wisconsin base.

We both decided to get married and live in his home state of Illinois. We planned to have a family and had four children, three sons and a daughter, and not in that order. My husband, their father, passed away at the age of forty six from cancer. On the day he died, March 15th, 1985 would of been our twenty fifth wedding anniversary.

When our children were all grown, and living on there own. And me at the the age of 51, I decided to sell my house in Illinois and purchase a house on Kentucky lake and move to Tennessee to live.

After purchasing the house on Kentucky lake, I acquired work cleaning homes for a couple of years to keep up on the mortgage of my new home until I could find better employment.

The beauty of Tennessee landscape, Kentucky lake and the laid back easiness of the people gave me enjoyment and inspiration to write poems. While I lived on Kentucky lake I happened to find other employment and then moved from the lake house to be closer to where I worked. I did not start writing poems again until six years later when I remarried.

Abandon Shed

An empty gray shed is crooked, weak, and abandon.
What was once useful, straight, and strong;
Now it stands with a slight lean
And, sometimes sounds off a groan.
It stands unexplained, deserted, and alone.

Tree

Firmly in the ground, I plant my roots.
I stand straight and tall.
My leaves bud green
In the spring,
And I change color in the fall.
My limbs reach
Toward the sky;
How I wish I could fly.

Even though I must remain
With my roots placed here
Planted firmly in the ground.

In the Hills of Tennessee

Mourning doves cooing, night owls hooting,
Ducks quaking, cranes swooping,
Eagles soaring, deer leaping,
Chipmunks scampering,
And a white-tailed fox dashes --
Into the rolling hills of Tennessee.

A Fall Day

Fall mornings have a chill in the air and a dense early morning mist that covers the ground; nestling itself among the trees, and lingering on the lake, and hovers over the bridge, giving an eerie mystical sense of fear as everything seems to disappear.

Then mid morning, sun rays stream through trees that have been long departed of their leaves and vanish the mist from the ground and all around.

Evening approaches, the setting sun has warmed and cleared the air and everything is still here. There was nothing to fear.

Tornado

Spinning, plucking all things up, tossing them around;
Hurling the broken pieces back down.
Tornado I say, "Spin yourself back around.
And leave us all here on the ground."

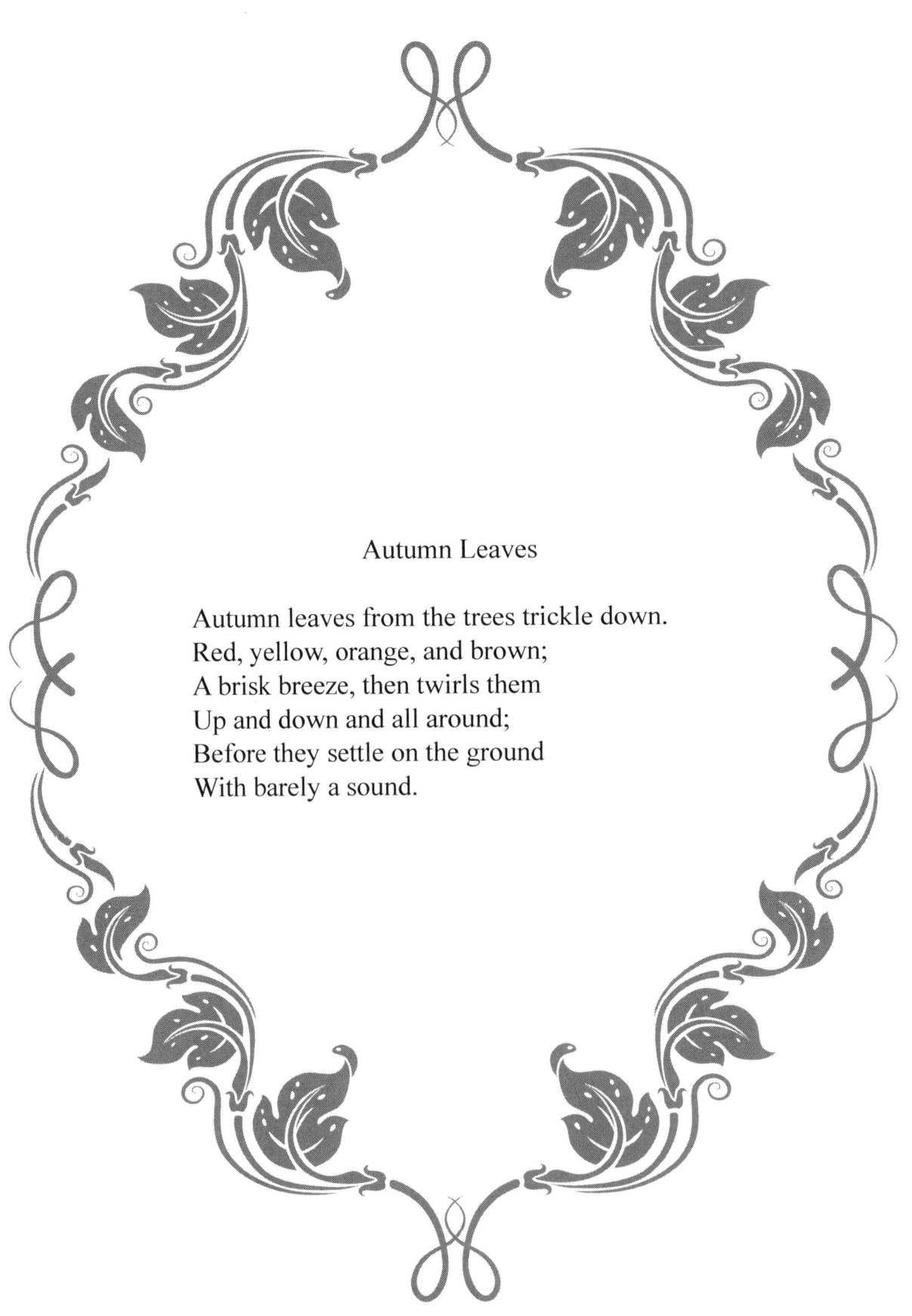

Autumn Leaves

Autumn leaves from the trees trickle down.
Red, yellow, orange, and brown;
A brisk breeze, then twirls them
Up and down and all around;
Before they settle on the ground
With barely a sound.

Lake Storm

Darkness in the sky and the sounds of booming thunder
Roll above and shake the ground. Wind gusts blowing,
making waves upon the lake and pushing them back
and forth. I do not shake for this storm wanes in its
wake upon the Kentucky lake.

Fathers

Fathers are enthusiastic about fishing, hunting, triathlons, and other outdoor sports.

A father is loving, caring, and benevolent. He endures with great vigilance while taking care of his family. When things go wrong, a father can be patient, helpful, and strong.

There is always a welcomed and needed place for him within all our indebted hearts.

Life a New

I feel the flutter of movement in my womb, the miracle of life a new, which is an unborn child physically connected to me as one, and I carry the new child with happiness and love. Then nine months will pass; our baby child grows as it stretches and pushes outward making more room for more growth.

New born of ours, your birth time has arrived. You will leave my womb and become a child. Then we will hold you close as you grow. You are our adorable newborn. Then we will embrace you and help you develop into adulthood and even when we may be extended apart we will always hold each other close in our heart.

A Sad Day

As I was driving home, from the grocery store, I passed you on the road. You looked lost and alone. While I drove on, I looked back at you in my review mirror. I could not look away. Your eyes reflected sadness. Your bones showed through your coat of fur. What a sad sight I thought you were.

I stopped the truck and backed it up, and I tore open a bag of dry dog food, which I had just purchased with my groceries. I proceeded to take a hand full out and laid it on the road. You ate it, but you would not come closer for more.

After discovering you were a female dog, I thought you might have had a litter of pups recently, so I coaxed you with a trail of dog food, hoping you would follow me home and stay. You would not abandon your offspring out of your love for them. Whether mammal or human, a mother's love is always there.

I never saw you again, and you haunt my thoughts of your suffering that day, and every day.

The Crossing

I had seen a female deer come out of the woods and then stand in the middle of a dirt road with her head held high.

Next she glanced up and down the road. Then to my surprise, from the woods, two spotted deer did appear.

I watched as I imagined the female deer to say, "Come, dear. Come, dear." Listen to your mother. It is safe to cross here, for I neither see nor do I smell any hunters near."

Then the two spotted fawns crossed over quickly to the other side by their mother and all then leaped into the woods and seemed to disappear.

My Bike

Pumping, pumping on my bike,
Pumping, pumping humming a song.
Glide, gliding, gliding along,
The air is cool, and I feel strong.
My bike and I are on our way,
We can play around all day.

My mother had said, "You may go out and play.
There are no chores for you to do today."

How Happy am I

The grass under my bare feet tickles my toes,
And the fragrance of a rose tickles my nose.
I look at the night sky and see the moon
And all the stars so high. Oh! So happy am I!

Sparky

I had a small dog named Sparky.
He was full of energy and did a lot of barking.
No barking in the house he was told.

Although, when he was let out
In the yard, he became very bold.
He would roll on the ground, jump up and down,
And have fun running all around.
Barking, barking, barking,
And barking.

I never scolded Sparky for barking in the yard.
Therefore, I would not scold him.

Lost Kitten

From the woods in Tennessee, came a frightened little kitten. I took you home with me. Wet, cold, and sick I cared for you every day; So you would become healthy and well to roam and play.

You had the strength and courage of a Lions heart. You fought a good fight for a new start. You were active each day until the sickness took you away. A friend buried you in the woods from where you came.

In the hills of Tennessee, under a strong Oak tree. I was smitten with you, for you were a brave little kitten.

Babe

My kitten named Babe leaps from a chair with neither heed nor care. She flies through the air with the greatest of ease, as if she were on a flying trapeze. Then she leaps to my curtains and with her claws she tries to hang on; it is then to her dismay that she will continue to slide all the way down to the floor. As she keeps complaining all the way, leaving herself and my curtains in total disarray.

I think. Should I give her away? No. I know that she is a kitten at play.

Coco

My dog Coco was as blond as he could be. Not the color of cocoa as anyone could plainly see. He could dance around on his two hind feet and spinning with glee to receive his treat."We would walk, run, and play care free all during the day." "He never let me out of his sight."

He is gone now. I miss him. He will always be more than a memory to me.

Patches My Aged Cat

My aged Calico cat, named Patches, has been with me a very long time. Despite her age and her slight limp, she is doing just fine.

She never adjusted to people or others of her kind. This difficulty in adapting was not hard to tell. When people and other animals would come into her view, she would hide out of sight; shivering, shaking, and becoming weary from fright.

Although, when everyone is asleep, Patches can now prowl and creep. Then she enjoys attacking toys on the floor and jumping onto the arm of a chair and lands precisely there with each of her feet. And all done with a flair, pouncing here and there.

My aged cat still has good sight and plays to her delight throughout the night. Then when she discovers no one is watching, she will jump up on my bed at night, and snuggle between my feet to have a good night sleep.

Paddy

My mixed chocolate lab named Paddy. She was a fine lassie. Brave? I think not!

She barked at almost anything she spotted.
And at night in the yard, even a tree gave her a great fright!

Though her eyes were bright and golden, her eyes expressed her moods of anger, disappointment, sadness, and surprise. Yet, above all, we shared between us a look of love.

Image of a Woman

Looking into the eyes of an older woman,
Where is the woman that I once new?
Age spots have replaced her faded freckles.
Now streaked with gray, the luster of her hair is gone. Days and months have turned into years that have slipped away. The time for living is growing short. There is a saying "Old too soon and smart too late".

Maybe, older and wiser with the acquired wisdom obtained throughout our life experiences.
I look at this older woman; I know her well - For the reflection in the mirror is my own.

Mirrored Images

Upon a body of water, the sun rays shine
Reflecting and resembling
Broken pieces of glass.

Twinkling stars as well, in the night sky,
Glitter upon the water
As glimmering pieces of diamonds.

The creator of heaven and earth
Gave us the sun and stars; so one may
Complement the other.

Spiders

Spiders webs are the strongest fiber known to humankind.
Spiders weave their webs on sheds, fences, cars, shrubs, trees,
And everywhere else they may please.
Spiders spin webs that float upon a breeze,
Then they spin their webs that get in my face and on my hair.
Spiders of the webs I try to sweep them away with a broom, but to my dismay
The spiders incredibly reappear and spin a new web the exact same day.
Spin your webs elsewhere to seek and catch your prey I say!

The Road

The traveled road with its highways and byways can be
made of dirt or can be black, gray, or copper in color.

They can be straight and narrow as an arrow
or twist and turn like a snake.

The roads go up the smallest of hills and to the highest
of mountains and down into the deepest valleys.

People drive in the dark of night or in the light of day,
and they try not to be caught on any roads that might
cause delay.

Whether we are traveling far and near, slow and fast, a
road will take us all where we have a plan to go.

Take Care

Our planet orbits in outer space;
It's holding us firmly in place.
It's taking care of our human race;
Our earth provides the air we breathe.
The food we eat, the water we drink,
And all the riches of our land by the directive plan.
We only need to look at the land
To see the wonder it provides;
Forest, streams, lakes, rivers and oceans wide.

Moon Man

Man in the moon in the sky with a cratered
face. Do you play "I Spy" with the other
Planets orbiting in outer space?

Kin and Kith

Our Kin and Kith. What a mix.
Nice to have when were in a fix.
So whom do we call? One, two, or all;
It would be difficult without any.
Whether Kin or Kith, we are there for one another.
Through the good times and sad times.
The only difference between them both is
That one is family. And the others are friends.

Time

Our lives revolve around clocks.
Tick. Tock. Tick. Tock.
We wake, eat, and sleep.
All to the sound of the time on the clock
Tick. Tock. Tick. Tock.
Let us go beyond the
Tick. Tock. Tick. Tock.
Set on the clock.

Let us pause - in the present -
And take a moment out of time,
For the joy of living and giving to others
And ourselves.

Days

Life is given, and life will slowly fade and be taken away. As days turn into weeks, and weeks turn into months. And, then into years. Time passes along albeit, as do our lives. We start to move more slowly as our height and stature begin to wither down. And, along with less energy - to no one's surprise. This day and every day seem to pass too quickly. The days that are left, I will welcome and make everyday an optimistic and encouraging day.

Look Be Aware

Look, look see all the colors.
See the different sizes and shapes?
Listen, listen closely, and hear the different sounds.
Can one describe what has been seen and heard?
If not, then look and listen again!
For beauty comes from without - and from within.
That's the human race.

Mutize

Ester was a lady who called me Mutize.
I asked, "Ester why do you call me Mutize?"
Please explain.
"I don't know," said Ester, in vain.
"You just look like a Mutize to me."
Mutize? So will the name bring me fame?
Can anyone explain?
I think it is just a silly odd nickname.

Tennessee

Tennessee is a great place to be. The sun is warm, the air is fresh, and there is the wilderness.

Eagles spread their magnificent wings and take flight. And start swooping and soaring against the bright blue sky.

Bands of ducks glide down and land on the lake as sea gulls just above flitter around.

Deer make their leaps and bounds as if in flight and land with only the sound of a snapping twig beneath their feet.

Our Land

Where are conversations on preservation, restoration, and appreciation for this land? Are we only filled with want and greed?

This earth supplies forests, lakes, rivers, and oceans; that provides for all our needs.

As we gauge out hillsides that expose harsh elements to tender tree roots that may not survive. The hand of humankind is pulluting rivers, oceans, lakes, streams, and the air we breathe.

Is this how we take care of our parent land, that provides us with all our needs?

Prayers

Prayers are central and vital to our human race.
We have even taken our prayers into outer space.

Praise and Adore

The Lord is with us in our hearts and souls.
So praise and adore him, please do not ignore him.
He has chosen all of human kind.
He is with us now and will be forevermore.

I hope reading these poems gave you pleasure.
May they be something you will treasure.

Poems are fun to write.
Some are true and right.

Others are way out of sight.
Surely none have given you a fright.

Authors Note:

When I made the move to Tennessee it enlighten my outlook.

There are states that we are born in, the ones we move to or we may visit. The culture may be different from state to state, but the people are the same in many ways.

Be pleasant and kind to those that live there and respectful of the state.

Let us not waste the time we have on earth. So it comes down to making a good life for ourselves and others and our pets with whatever time is allotted to us while were here.

Poems ?
Poems ?
Poems ?
Poems ?
Poems ?
?

Made in the USA
Lexington, KY
06 March 2018